Clockwise

First published in Great Britain in 1999 by Macdonald Young Books

Macdonald Young Books,
an imprint of Wayland Publishers Ltd
61 Western Road
Hove, East Sussex
BN3 1JD

© Macdonald Young Books 1999
Text © Sam Godwin 1999
Illustrations © Anthony Lewis 1999
M.Y.Bees artwork © Clare Mackie

Commissioning Editor: Dereen Taylor
Editor: Lisa Edwards
Designer: Rebecca Elgar
Language Consultant: Dr Carol Ballard
Creature Consultant: Stephen Savage

A CIP catalogue for this book is available from the British Library
Printed and bound in Portugal by Edições ASA

ISBN 0 7500 2664 2

Clockwise

Sam Godwin

Illustrated by
Anthony Lewis

MACDONALD YOUNG BOOKS

Tick...tick...tick.
Time is ticking away.

Time flies.

We use the word **time** all the time.

But how do we measure time?

The smallest unit of time you can measure on a clock is a second.

In 1 second, a hummingbird flaps its wings 78 times.

That gives us just enough time to jump in the air once!

The second hand measures seconds.
It moves forward 1 mark every second.

Penguin feeding
time: 1.30pm

A watch like this one
is a clock you wear
on your wrist.

You can see the seconds marked
around the edge of the clock.
There are 60 of them.

Sixty seconds make one minute.

In 1 minute, a cheetah can run 4 times round a race track.

Wow!

In 1 hour the minute hand moves
once round the clock.

At the same time, the hour hand moves
forward from 1 number to the next.
The numbers count the hours.

13

There are 5 minute marks between each number.

Count them and you will find out how many minutes past the hour it is.

15

Seven days make one week.

You can see the days of the week marked
on a diary or a calendar.
Each day has its own name.

MONDAY

TUESDAY

WEDNESDAY

THURSDAY

FRIDAY

SATURDAY

SUNDAY

Thirty or thirty-one days make one month.

In 1 month, a caterpillar changes into a butterfly.

In the same time, your hair grows 1 centimetre longer.

Each month has a different name. You can see them on this calendar. Some months have 30 days, others have 31 days. February usually has 28 days but every 4 years it has 29.

JANUARY

M	T	W	T	F	S	S
		1	2	3	4	5
6	7	8	9	10	11	12
13	14	15	16	17	18	19
20	21	22	23	24	25	26
27	28	29	30	31		

FEBRUARY

M	T	W	T	F	S	S
					1	2
3	4	5	6	7	8	9
10	11	12	13	14	15	16
17	18	19	20	21	22	23
24	25	26	27	28		

MARCH

M	T	W	T	F	S	S
					1	2
3	4	5	6	7	8	9
10	11	12	13	14	15	16
17	18	19	20	21	22	23
24	25	26	27	28	29	30
31						

APRIL

M	T	W	T	F	S	S
	1	2	3	4	5	6
7	8	9	10	11	12	13
14	15	16	17	18	19	20
21	22	23	24	25	26	27
28	29	30				

MAY

M	T	W	T	F	S	S
		1	2	3	4	
5	6	7	8	9	10	11
12	13	14	15	16	17	18
19	20	21	22	23	24	25
26	27	28	29	30	31	

JUNE

M	T	W	T	F	S	S
						1
2	3	4	5	6	7	8
9	10	11	12	13	14	15
16	17	18	19	20	21	22
23	24	25	26	27	28	29
30						

JULY

M	T	W	T	F	S	S
	1	2	3	4	5	6
7	8	9	10	11	12	13
14	15	16	17	18	19	20
21	22	23	24	25	26	27
28	29	30	31			

AUGUST

M	T	W	T	F	S	S
				1	2	3
4	5	6	7	8	9	10
11	12	13	14	15	16	17
18	19	20	21	22	23	24
25	26	27	28	29	30	31

SEPTEMBER

M	T	W	T	F	S	S
1	2	3	4	5	6	7
8	9	10	11	12	13	14
15	16	17	18	19	20	21
22	23	24	25	26	27	28
29	30					

OCTOBER

M	T	W	T	F	S	S
	1	2	3	4	5	
6	7	8	9	10	11	12
13	14	15	16	17	18	19
20	21	22	23	24	25	26
27	28	29	30	31		

NOVEMBER

M	T	W	T	F	S	S
					1	2
3	4	5	6	7	8	9
10	11	12	13	14	15	16
17	18	19	20	21	22	23
24	25	26	27	28	29	30

DECEMBER

M	T	W	T	F	S	S
1	2	3	4	5	6	7
8	9	10	11	12	13	14
15	16	17	18	19	20	21
22	23	24	25	26	27	28
29	30	31				

Twelve months make one year.

In 1 year, a baby giraffe grows about 100 centimetres or 1 metre.

You grow about 6 centimetres taller.

Every year is given a number.
This helps people remember when
things happened.

What year were you born in?

One hundred years make a century.

If you put the name
and number of a day

THURSDAY 14

next to the name
of a month

AUGUST

and the number
of a year

1997

you get a date

THURSDAY, 14 AUGUST 1997

Do you know your own date of birth?

25

Ten centuries make one millenium.

27

Look at the time!

A sun dial is a very old kind of stone clock. You can tell what time it is by checking where the sun's shadow falls. The time on this sun dial is 3 o' clock.

▼

▲

A grandfather clock has a part called a pendulum. It swings backwards and forwards to show that the clock is working properly. It makes a loud ticking sound as well.

An alarm clock wakes you up in the morning. Some alarm clocks have a loud ring or buzzer. Others have a radio.

You wear a wristwatch on a strap around your wrist. You can tell the time wherever you are.

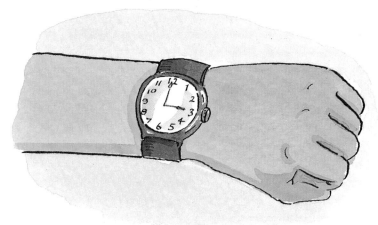

An hour glass measures time by letting sand slip from the top part of it to the lower part.

GLOSSARY

DAY
A length of time lasting 24 hours. Part of a day is in darkness and part in daylight.

MONTH
A length of time made up of 30 or 31 days. One month, February, is different. It has 28 days, and every four years it has 29 days. There are 12 months in one year.

UNIT
A fixed amount of something. For example, the second is a unit of time.

HOUR
A length of time made up of 60 minutes. There are 24 hours in one day.

SECOND
A very short length of time. There are 60 seconds in one minute.

WEEK
A length of time made up of 7 days.

MINUTE
A short length of time made up of 60 seconds. There are 60 minutes in one hour.

TIME
We know that time passes by the way days and nights repeat themselves or the movement of the hands on a clock. We measure time by using units such as seconds, minutes and hours.

YEAR
A length of time made up of 12 months, or 52 weeks, or 365 days.